The Smoky God
The Mysteries of the Inner Earth

Table of Contents

Chapter 1. Introduction

Embark on an unprecedented journey to the heart of planet earth, diving into the mysteries that lie beneath our feet in our special report, "The Smoky God: The Mysteries of the Inner Earth". This enchanting piece of investigative journalism, brimming with intrigue, takes you to unexplored territories, where the sun is said to shine in polar darkness, and civilizations undiscovered potentially thrive. From ancient myths to modern-day theories, our narrative unveils a realm that has fascinated the human imagination for millennia. No special scientific background is required; your curiosity is the only passport needed! So tread into the unseen, and who knows, you might find the earth is far more multi-layered than you ever imagined! Explore, enjoy, and immerse yourself in this spectacular journey towards the center under our feet. This Special Report, delightfully written and meticulously researched, just might be the intellectual adventure you need! So why wait? With "The Smoky God: The Mysteries of the Inner Earth", prepare to look at our world in a whole new light.

Chapter 2. Setting the Stage: History of Hollow Earth Theories

In an exploration as enthralling as our venture into the hollow earth theories, it seems fitting to first delve into the depths of human history, where our fascination with the realms beneath our feet took root. Throughout history, from the time of the ancient civilizations to the modern age, the concept of a Hollow Earth has shifted, evolved, and intertwined with our understanding of the universe.

2.1. Ancient Hickory and the Roots of Belief

Our story commences in the vaults of ancient history where the seeds of the Hollow Earth concept were first planted, albeit in a spectral and metaphysical form. The Greek realm of Hades, the Norse underworld of Hel, and the Christian concept of Hell are representative of early human societies' perspectives of a mysterious world under the Earth's crust.

The Greeks, for instance, believed in the existence of Hades, a shadowy beneath-the-surface realm that housed the souls of the departed. Similarly, ancient Norse cosmology presented a complex underworld—Svartálfheim (home of the dwarves) and Hel (abode of those who did not die heroically)—profoundly rooted beneath the "Tree of Life," Yggdrasil. Furthermore, in Christian belief, Hell, envisioned as an enormous infernal realm deep under Earth's surface, houses sinners, prompting a spiritual perspective of what lies under the crust.

2.2. Pivotal Shifts: The Renaissance and the Enlightenment

Fast-forwarding to the Renaissance, our notions about the world began to crystallize under the lens of scientific rigor and exploration. Intriguing parallels can be drawn from Dante Alighieri's "Divine Comedy" – where he traverses through Hell, Purgatory and Paradise. Even though fundamentally fictitious and theological, Dante's depiction of the underground world bears striking similarity to Hollow Earth theories that would later surface during the Enlightenment.

In the 17th century, the great astronomer Edmond Halley, after whom Halley's comet is named, posited a revolutionary idea. Drawing from his research into anomalous compass readings, Halley posited that the Earth was a hollow shell composed of four concentric spheres, each boasting its own magnetic field. Halley suggested that the space within these spherical shells might be inhabitable and potentially illuminated by a diffuse, ethereal light, a notion reminiscent of ancient mythologies.

2.3. The Flames of Novelty: 18th to 20th Century

This era saw Hollow Earth theories take a more solid form, shaped by the scientific advances of the time. A noteworthy contributor to the concept from this era was John Cleves Symmes Jr. In the early 19th century, Symmes fervently campaigned for the theory of a hollow Earth featuring openings at the poles. His tireless advocacy led to the U.S. Congress seriously considering an expedition to one of the poles, albeit the venture never materialized.

In the vein of intriguing theories, Cyrus Teed surfaced in the later part of the 19th century with his ideas of "Cellular Cosmogony" or the

Koreshan Unity. He proposed that we live on the interior of the Earth's shell, a stark reversal of standard understanding of the cosmos. This idea was the backdrop of a utopian community he founded in Florida, committing to the belief and further developing the lore of the Hollow Earth for years.

Exploring the 20th century, Richard E. Byrd, a celebrated American naval officer and polar explorer, has often been associated, albeit contentiously, with Hollow Earth theories. Some believers cite undisclosed diary entries from Byrd, claiming that he discovered lush, habitable lands during a polar exploration.

2.4. Through the Lens of Popular Culture

The Hollow Earth concept has also seeped into popular culture, served as fodder for science fiction and fantasy. From Edgar Rice Burroughs's Pellucidar series, where an inner world is housed at the Earth's core – to modern blockbusters like "Journey to the Center of the Earth" and the "Godzilla vs. Kong," the notion of the Hollow Earth has been an inextricable part of our cultural consciousness.

Pop culture is a reflection of societal sentiments, fears, and fascinations. The persistent presence of Hollow Earth concepts within it is a testimony to the timeless allure of unexplored realms and mysteries.

Our trajectory through the echelons of history, charting the evolution of Hollow Earth theories, is the perfect prologue to our exploration. We've charted the path from spiritual and ideological platforms to hypotheses grounded in nascent scientific understanding. These theories, as diverse as they are fascinating and controversial, lay the foundation for our deeper dive into the mysteries held within the depths of our planet.

Chapter 3. Probing the Legend: 'The Smoky God' in Detail

The mysteries of our world are manifold, yet there are a select few that continue to defy our understanding and challenge our paradigms. One such enigma is the legend of 'The Smoky God'. Filled with intrigue, this beguiling account takes us into the entrails of our earth, presenting a reality that seems both tangible and otherworldly.

3.1. Origin

The "Smoky God" narrative originates from a forgotten piece of literature published in 1908. Titled 'The Smoky God, or A Voyage to the Inner World,' its author, Willis George Emerson, transcribed the almost fantastical testament of a Norwegian seafarer, Olaf Jansen. According to Jansen, he and his father Jens embarked on an extraordinary sojourn into the hollow interior of the earth, an experience that seems plucked from the grandeur of mythology than the concreteness of reality.

3.2. The Encounter

A frail old man, Jansen, shared his incredible tale with Emerson on his deathbed. Jansen's narrative began when he and his father set sail from Stockholm, intending to catch and store fish in the Arctic Ocean. Their journey, however, transformed into a skin-of-the-teeth survival tale when violent storms misdirected them into the thick fog, intense cold, and icy waters for many days. When the fog finally lifted, they found themselves navigating a warm river leading towards a radiant 'inner sun': an entity they later named 'The Smoky God' due to its smoky-red hue.

3.3. The Inner Earth Civilization

As they journeyed further in, they discovered a rich, thriving environment, teeming with lush vegetation and exotic wildlife, some of which were mammoth in size, stoking tales of extinct creatures still roaming free. Most strikingly, they allegedly interacted with the inhabitants of this inner world. The denizens, described as being physically larger and technologically advanced, apparently treated them with kindness. An organised and peaceful society, they lived in cities constructed from precious stones, bathed in the warm glow of the inner sun that illuminated their world.

3.4. Scepticism and Scientific Analysis

From a scientific standpoint, the hollow earth theory and the existence of an 'inner sun' brooks much scepticism. The field of geology, earth's internal structures, and seismic activities have categorically denied these possibilities. Earth's inner core, as far as contemporary science is concerned, is a solid ball of iron-nickel alloy, subjected to extreme pressure and heat - no giant inner sun or civilizations could possibly survive under such conditions. Yet the Jansen narrative forces us to question whether our scientific understanding is absolute or if there could be anomalies that have not yet fallen into the domain of our knowledge.

3.5. The Hollow Earth Hypothesis

Despite such scepticism, the concept of a hollow earth has found resonation across various epochs. Ancient civilizations from Greeks to Hindus to Mayans have their versions of subterranean realms, often places of deities or ancestral spirits. So persistent is this belief that in the 17th century, the celebrated astronomer and mathematician, Sir Edmond Halley, postulated that the earth is made of several concentric shells, enclosing within them luminous atmospheres capable of supporting life.

Jansen's narrative brings these ancient beliefs into consideration. Could his 'inner earth,' rather than being an absurd fantasy, be a real and verifiable place? A place existing not just in the realm of myths and legends but couched snugly in the proximity of our physical world?

3.6. Towards the Unseen

While we stand on the brink of such cosmic questions, our curiosity compels us to delve deeper, process the improbable, and probe the uncanny. 'The Smoky God' story, thus, serves not just as a fantastical account but as a reminder of the human penchant for exploration - a drive that propels us towards the unseen, the unverified, and the unknown.

In conclusion, the enigmatic nature of the 'The Smoky God' legend serves as a fascinating lens through which we can re-examine our own understanding of the world. While sceptical minds may shrug it off as the deathbed hallucinations of an old man, it remains a narrative worth scrutinising. The tale serves as an allegory, urging us to probe the deepest realms of our existence and bask in the transcendent majesty of cosmic curiosity.

Chapter 4. The Science Behind the Myth: Geological Perspectives

Our trek into the heart of Mother Earth commences at the surface, where we stand on what we know and trust. Earth's skin, the crust, is a patchwork, a mosaic of plates that are ever-shuffling, crashing, and drifting over the gargantuan time scales of geological eras.

4.1. The Earth's Geology: Not Lost in Translation

Envision the Earth as an enormous machine, tirelessly working over billions of years, crafting mountains, valleys, and oceans, painting landscapes that would take the breath away from the most hardened cynics. Everything we perceive around us is the product of the Earth's unceasing labor - the consequence of plate tectonics. This idea is a relatively contemporary one, the term 'plate tectonics' having been coined only towards the late 1960s. It provides a framework to understand the geological processes that shaped and continue to shape our world.

Let's consider the Earth's structure. We are all familiar with the basic model: the crust where we live, the mantle beneath, and then the metallic core at the center. The crust, distinctively lighter than the other layers, is made up of major continental plates and several minor ones, spanning across oceans and landmasses. These plates float on the denser, semi-fluid mantle beneath.

The mantle, stretching roughly 2900 kilometers beneath our feet, composed predominantly of silicate rocks, is the engine of this planetary machine. The heat coming from the core causes the semi-molten rocks in the mantle to convect, setting up an enormous conveyer belt of rock and heat. This movement of molten rock propels the tectonic plates, dividing, colliding, and grinding against each other.

4.2. Hollow Earth: A Conjecture's Journey Through Time

Would it surprise you to find out that the theory of a hollow Earth, that we are mere surface dwellers of a planet teeming with life in subterranean halls, finds its roots in antiquity? Various cultures around the world harbor folklore that speaks of entire civilizations thriving beneath our feet. From the Greeks who believed in the Underworld ruled by Hades, to the Hindu cosmology of Patala, whose seven realms of snake-like beings exist beneath the surface, the narratives are colorful and diverse.

In a more recent take, Edmund Halley of the Halley's Comet fame postulated that the Earth was made up of concentric shells, separated by individual atmospheres, each shell capable of supporting life. His deductions were rooted in the irregularities in Earth's magnetic field, which he attributed to the movements of these shells. Leonhard Euler, the venerated Swiss mathematician, simplified Halley's model, proposed a single hollow Earth with a central sun providing warmth and light.

These postulates, intriguing as they are, do not comply with our contemporary understanding of geology and the vast amount of data we have accumulated. The concept of gravity, seismic activity, the Earth's magnetosphere - all point towards a solid and dynamic Earth, rather than a hollow one. And while we cannot bore into the Earth and see for ourselves, we can read the signs she willingly offers, and piece together a more realistic, albeit less mythical, image of what lies beneath.

4.3. Seismic Evidence: Earth's Autopsy Report

Seismic waves provide a substantial corpus of evidence that helps us understand the Earth's inner structure. Generated during earthquakes, these waves journey through the Earth, getting reflected, refracted, and bent, as they encounter materials of different densities. Two types of waves are of particular interest to us: P-waves that move in a push-pull manner, like slinky, and S-waves, which shake the ground perpendicularly to their travel direction.

P-waves, which travel faster, can traverse through both solid and liquid media. S-waves, on the other hand, can pass only through solids. This gives us an important clue about the structure of Earth's core. The shadow zones, where seismic waves are not detected during an earthquake, suggest the presence of a solid core and a liquid outer core, thereby ruling out the possibility of a hollow Earth.

4.4. The Gravity of the Situation: Down to Earth Facts

Gravity, that fundamental force that keeps us tethered to the surface, provides yet another key to debunk the hollow Earth theory. Simply put, it is the force of attraction that every mass exerts on every other mass. The heavier the mass, the stronger the gravitational force. If indeed, the Earth were hollow, the gravitational pull we experience on the surface would be drastically reduced.

Furthermore, Earth's mass and volume are calculable, thereby enabling calculations of its overall density —about 5.5 grams per cubic centimeter. This figure aligns well with our understanding of the Earth's layered structure and contradicts the likely significantly lower density of a hollow Earth.

As we dive deeper into the mysteries of our planet, it becomes compellingly clear that while the hollow Earth concept fascinates us, our current understanding of nature and the physical world tells a different tale. But, in a realm where truth may indeed be stranger than fiction, our journey is far from over!

Chapter 5. The Core of Controversy: Debunking and Validations

Throughout history, as mariners charted new routes and explorers set foot on unknown lands, thoughts always drifted towards the unexplored, the uncharted, and the unseen. The inner earth, hidden beneath miles of crust and mantle, has stayed among the list of the less explored terrains. The idea of a hollow earth itself has stirred heated debates and triggered scientific inquiries, dismissing some theories while validating others with verifiable facts.

5.1. Hollow Earth Theory: Historical Views to Modern Interpretations

The Hollow Earth Theory may sound like a modern invention fabricated by science fiction enthusiasts, but its roots date back to ancient mythologies and traditions. There was an essential belief in multiple cultures worldwide that the earth was hollow, housing a different world or even different civilizations within its belly.

Early proponents, inspired by these myths and legends, included Edmund Halley, who proposed a hollow earth model in the late 17th century. His model consisted of a series of concentric shells within the interior of the earth, each one housing its life mechanisms.

Despite being based on Halley's attempts to account for geomagnetic anomalies, this theory has since been dismissed. Modern science confirms this with empirical data, demonstrating that the earth is anything but hollow. However, the theory still captivates imaginations and has fueled countless works of fiction and fringe scientific theories.

5.2. A Solid Stand: Proving Earth's Solidity

Our understanding of the earth's interior is mostly based on the study of seismic waves, which are generated by earthquakes. These waves travel through the Earth's layers, changing speed at every boundary they encounter, which allows scientists to map the physical properties of our planet's innards.

The delayed arrival of some types of seismic waves at seismograph stations across the globe indicates the presence of a liquid outer core. These interpretations directly oppose the Hollow Earth Theory.

Reinforcing these findings, the study of gravitational force and its balance also provides us clues disproving the hollow Earth concept. If the earth were hollow, there would be less mass and thus less gravity. Equations compiled from Newton's laws of motion starkly undermine the hollow earth concept and support the established structure of a solid planet with a core, mantle, and crust.

5.3. Inner Earth Life: A Quandary of Biological Possibilities

The fantasy of another civilization living within the Earth's bowels has been a staple of stories and legends. While it remains just that – a fantasy – in the context of a hollow world, the idea of life deep within our solid Earth holds a bit of a quandary.

Subsurface biosphere studies have revealed microorganisms residing several kilometers below the Earth's surface, thriving in harsh conditions that would otherwise be deemed uninhabitable. This tantalizing discovery does, in a way, verify the existence of an 'Inner Earth life,' albeit not with the grandeur associated with the Hollow Earth Theory.

Should these hypothetical underground residents have developed in the crushing pressures and blazing temperatures of deeper, still unexplored reaches, they would certainly be very different from any life form we know. But this remains a matter of scientific speculation until further research and exploration bring us conclusive evidence.

Adding to the controversy, some scientists even propose the existence of Lost Civilizations residing in underground labyrinths. While evidences for this are scant and often speculative, these theories do spark intrigue and are worth following as part of the ongoing narrative of Inner Earth mysteries.

5.4. Conclusion: Navigating Amidst Fact & Fiction

A fine line separates fact from fiction when it comes to the mysteries of the Inner Earth. Science has debunked the Hollow Earth Theory, showing us that our planet is more of a layered cake than a hollow shell. On the other hand, the idea of life in the depths is not entirely unfounded, offering exciting possibilities for future exploration.

In summation, the core of the earth brings with it debates and controversy, rigorous scientific inquiry, and imaginative pondering. It's a subject that ceaselessly intrigues, prompts deep thought, and spurs our creative imaginings. From acknowledging the wild and improbable to considering the credible, we traverse the spectrum of inner earth possibilities in our collective quest for knowledge. The more we know, the closer we come to unveiling the mysteries of the Inner Earth.

For now, the journey continues, leading us deeper into the intriguing layers of the planet we call home. While science provides us with factual landmarks, our imagination conjures up fantastical routes and destinations, making the exploration of the Inner Earth an expedition unlike any other.

In parting, may these revelations lead not to fixed conclusions but foster a desire for continual exploration, an insatiable curiosity about what lies beneath our feet, and a relentless pursuit of truths wrapped in layers of solid, fiery, and enigmatic earth, ever inviting, ever mysterious.

The journey to the heart of planet Earth continues.

Chapter 6. Architects of Imagination: Hollow Earth in Literature and Popular Culture

Our quest begins, not with scientific inquiries or dazzling claims of travellers lost, but within the realm of dreams woven intricately by the architects of imagination, those we often affectionately term as writers and artists. As conceivable by human imagination so is its manifestation, and thus, quite naturally, literature and popular culture have often grappled with the idea of a world beneath our crusty trampoline of habitable land. Fascinating fictional narratives, comic book adventures, cinematic tales or even video games, each have been a platform where the concept of Hollow Earth has found fruitful terrain.

6.1. The Literary Landscape

We journey first into the captivating depth of the written word, where the unending expanse of possibilities has given birth to the most enduring and celebrated tales of Hollow Earth. It was writers who initially popularized the concept, with tales of secret passages leading to a subterranean world teeming with life and hidden wonders.

Among the earliest, Ludvig Holberg's "Niels Klim's Underground Travels" woven in 1741, narrates the adventures of the protagonist Niels who falls into a cave and reaches an underground utopia of tree people. Another work, "Symzonia; Voyage of Discovery" published anonymously in 1820, recounts the voyage to a hollow world entered through the North and South poles. Some scholars suggest that the author is potentially John Cleves Symmes Jr., an army officer who was a proponent of hollow Earth theory, lending the work its captious title.

In Edgar Allan Poe's narrative "The Narrative of Arthur Gordon Pym of Nantucket", the protagonist and his crew inadvertently reach the inner earth, hinted at being peopled and full of mysteries, reaffirming the trope of the hollow Earth concept. But perhaps the most influential literary work that intrigues the realm of hollow Earth is Jules Verne's enduring classic, "Journey to the Centre of the Earth". Verne's creation teems with prehistoric life and fantastic subterranean vistas, endearing its concept to the hearts of millions of readers worldwide.

6.2. Journey Through Popular Culture

Like the iconic stalagmites and stalactites of underground caves, literature deeply influences the formation of cultural stalactites or trends that drip into and proliferate in popular culture. Hollow Earth, thus, didn't remain confined to the written word for long, but seeped into celluloid, radio waves, and pixelated forms, finding further fertile grounds for its conceptual propagation.

On the silver screen, variations of the trope abound. The 2008 film "Journey to the Center of the Earth", inspired by Verne's novel, carries the theme forward with modern cinematic techniques. The Godzilla franchise too, hints at the existence of an Underworld: 'Hollow Earth', where these gigantic creatures originate. Harold Ramis' "Year One" displays an earth that opens up showcasing prehistoric worlds, while "At the Earth's Core" brings us fauna of the hollow Earth.

In the realm of radio and TV, shows like "Doctor Who" have utilized the trope frequently, with entire civilizations and ecosystems thriving beneath the surface of the Earth. Video games, with their immersive worlds, have handily adopted Hollow Earth themes, offering players the chance to explore mythical landscapes and encounter unusual creatures. "ARK: Survival Evolved", "Terraria" and "Final Fantasy IV", present players with such unique experiences.

6.3. Impact on Society and Future Trends

Although largely a work of creation from the architects of imagination, the hollow Earth concept has greatly influenced societal perceptions and interests concerning our planet. The enduring fascination with inner space has fueled countless expeditions and scientific investigations, propelling advancements in geology and exploration technologies.

What lies in the future for this concept? Perhaps as our understanding of the universe expands, which routinely rebuffs the presuppositions of the past, the hollow Earth will morph and adapt. Whether as a labyrinth of tunnels hosting alien life or a refuge for humans in a post-apocalyptic world, our perception is only limited by the boundaries of our imagination.

In conclusion, spanning literature to popular culture, the hollow Earth theory has been weaved into the fabric of human intellectual pursuits and creative expression. Though its scientific verity is absent or limited, its influence has certainly permeated deep, positively shaping our curiosity about the world beneath us.

Chapter 7. The Unseen Realm: Mapping the Inner Earth

Unraveling the threads of mythology, archaeology, and pseudoscience that hint at a world beneath our world is far from an easy task. From the ancient tales of subterranean Shambhala and Agartha, to the quirky Hollow Earth theories popularized in the 19th century, to the astonishing geological discoveries of recent decades, the possibility of an Inner Earth has captivated curiosities and inspired imaginings.

7.1. The Mythical Roots of the Inner Earth

Every civilization, it seems, eventually stumbles upon the idea of a hidden realm; a secret world right beneath our feet. Myths from countless cultures speak in hushed whispers about a mysterious subterranean abode.

Among the Tibetan Buddhists, the myth of Shambhala, a hidden kingdom in the deepest recesses of the Himalayas, has been told for centuries. For adherents of ancient Hindu philosophy, there is talk of the holy city of Agartha, existing somewhere beneath the surface of our earth, filled with hidden wisdom and celestial knowledge. These stories extend to Native American folklore as well. Indeed, the Hopi tribe recounts the history of their ancestors emerging from an underground world into the dazzling daylight of our own earth.

7.2. The Giants of Modern Theory

While theories of an Inner Earth might seem the stuff of ancient legend and New Age mysticism, they have largely been stoked by figures from the modern West. Early proponents included John Cleves Symmes Jr, an American ex-army officer who, drawing from the works of earlier mystical writers, insisted that our planet housed a hollow interior with gaping polar entrances. Edmund Halley, the astronomer famed for calculating the orbit of Halley's Comet, also speculated that the Earth might consist of several concentric shells separated by individual atmospheres, each potentially housing life of its own.

7.3. The Legacy of The Smoky God

Perhaps the most fascinating tale came in the early 20th century, with the publication of Willis George Emerson's 'The Smoky God', which narrative this very report is primarily based on. Purportedly based on the real-life experiences of Norwegian sailor Olaf Jansen, it tells of a journey through the North Pole into a hollow Earth populated by 12-foot tall beings who worshipped the smoky central sun, hence 'The Smoky God'. The book, mingling fact and fiction, set the foundations for the modern day fascination in this field, and its legacy endures till date in the form of a cult following.

7.4. Converting Speculation to Science

Modern science was mostly dismissive of these theories until the twentieth century. The advent of seismic science and the use of seismic waves started giving researchers surprising insights into the Earth's inner structure. The extensive underground seismic-activity recording enabled scientists to make accurate maps of Earth's internal structure. The Earth, they found, is not hollow but consists of multiple layers—crust, mantle, outer core, and inner core. Each layer exhibits unique properties. Seismic waves allowed us to find out more about these structures, their composition, and their influence on Earth's magnetism.

However, the real jaw-dropper perhaps is the latest idea emerging from the quantum mechanical estimates. Extracting theories from the realm of abstract mathematics, some modern theorists propose that there may exist entire civilizations, not just beneath our feet, but interpenetrating our reality on frequencies beyond human perception— a hidden realm co-existing on our plain of existence.

Thus, the mystical tales of ancient sages, the dreams of eccentric 19th-century thinkers, the seismic revelations of twentieth-century science, and the multidimensional speculations of 21st-century quantum theory do not point to a singular truth. They reveal instead an array of possibilities, of readings of the Earth and the Universe that are as layered and as enchanting as the stories and studies that inspire them.

While we may be some way off from conclusively establishing the existence of an Inner Earth civilization, the journey we embark on while seeking to answer this question takes us on a fascinating roller-coaster ride through the realm of human curiosity and creativity. This legacy, so deeply rooted in our collective ethos, emerges through various forms over time and is therein lies the real spellbinding enigma of the 'Inner Earth'.

Ultimately, whether the Inner Earth is a physical reality or just the product of fertile imaginations, it provides a unique mirror, reflecting humanity's relentless quest for knowledge and our tongue tied awe of the mysteries that surround us. As such, our search for the 'Inner Earth' says perhaps less about the unseen layers of our planet and more about the curious, questioning, and ever-expanding nature of our minds.

Chapter 8. Beyond the Poles: Astonishing Claims and Anecdotes

Standing at the edges of the earth, paint a mental picture of the mighty poles, a visual symphony of nature's grandeur - resplendent in their frosty charm, a timeless enigma that has long baffled and captivated humankind. Often seen as immovable sentinels, standing defiant against the ravages of time and unflinching under the harshest environmental conditions, the poles have been the epicenter of numerous groundbreaking exploration attempts. But, perhaps their biggest secret that continues to create ripples in our collective minds, is the possibility of them being gateways to an internal world hidden beneath vast expanses of ice and snow.

8.1. Expedition Anecdotes: Early Intriguing Observations

Noted with careful precision by explorers braving the polar terrains, several puzzling occurrences suggest a realm alien to everything we thought we understood about Earth's design. Remarkably, these anomalies often coincide with specific geographic latitudes.

A striking instance is the documented journey of English explorer James Clark Ross, who in 1841, while navigating the Antarctic, came across an irregular composition of the magnetic field that befuddled compass readings. This mysterious variation, labeled the 'magnetic dip,' intensified as Ross moved towards what was then considered the South Magnetic Pole - a possible indication of an unseen geographic feature, possibly even an entrance to an inner world.

Around the same time, incidents of 'warm winds' were reported by polar explorers at distinctly high latitudes, both in the Arctic and Antarctic regions. These warm winds, a seeming aberration considering the generally frigid climates, propelled the theory of a warmer, habitable region lying beneath.

Such peculiarities were not limited to the frozen landscapes. Sicilian explorer Luigi Palmieri, during an expedition to Mount Vesuvius in 1858, observed anomalous seismic activity. The fascinating pattern, unlike typical earthquake activity, appeared to originate from not above or beneath the crater, but from within – as if from a world inside.

8.2. The Symmes Hollow Earth Theory

If one delves into the realm of conjectures, the Symmes Hollow Earth Theory, proposed by American officer John Cleves Symmes Jr., is particularly noteworthy. Claiming the existence of enormous holes at the poles, he suggested they serve as entrances to the earth's interior, potentially sheltering advanced civilizations.

Symmes even lobbied for an expedition to penetrate these polar openings, attracting considerable attention in the early 19th century. Although the planned voyage never came to fruition, his theories continue to stimulate imaginations, sparking off numerous literary works and forming the bedrock for further speculative hypotheses.

8.3. The Antarctic Odyssey of Admiral Byrd

Perhaps the most widely discussed episode linked to polar penetration narratives is the Antarctic voyage of Admiral Richard E. Byrd, an American naval officer. In his log detailing the 1947 Operation Highjump, Byrd reportedly flew over the South Pole into an area hidden from the rest of the world.

His account, however, takes an incredible turn when he describes flying into a 'warm,' 'green,' 'oasis-like' region instead of the ice landscapes one would typically expect. Although academically unverified, Byrd's testament arguably stands as the most substantial claim reinforcing the hollow earth theory.

8.4. A Portal to the Inner Earth: Modern Claims and Conjectures

Even as we march forward in the 21st century, old legends continue to rub shoulders with modern curiosity. With the advent of satellite technology, some speculate that certain photographic blanks in polar regions indicate deliberate masking of information, possibly to hide entrances leading to the inner Earth.

Meanwhile, the scientific community continues probing the mysteries under our feet with advanced seismology equipment. Recent discoveries of cavernous voids underneath the Antarctic sheet ice and a 660-km deep 'discontinuity' within the upper mantle, captured by Princeton geophysicists, keep stoking the fires of our imaginations.

Remember, the journey towards an understanding of our planet is ceaseless. Whether the poles are gateways to a new underground world or just monoliths of ice and rock continues to spark debate among the most brilliant minds. In every puzzle piece that we uncover, we stride a bit more towards understanding the grand tapestry of our existence.

While the conjectures and anecdotes surrounding what lies beyond the poles may lack empirical evidence, they stimulate dialogue, driving mankind's insatiable quest for knowledge. The poles, with their majestic allure, will continue to command intrigue, spinning narratives around their mysterious, potentially multi-layered structure. After all, the most fantastic aspect of exploration is the thrill of encountering the incredible unknown.

Chapter 9. Scientific U-turns: The Evolution of Inner Earth Theories

The study of our planet's interior isn't new. From the ancient conception of a hollow earth to the contemporary understanding of a dynamic, multi-layered geosphere, our perception of what lies beneath our feet has evolved tremendously over time. In this odyssey, humanity has made several scientific U-turns, revising theories and scrutinizing evidence in pursuit of truth.

9.1. The Primordial Beliefs

There's no better place to start than at the very beginning, tracing theories back to ancient times when myths outshone science. The concept of an inner earth has roots in ancient folklore, mythology, and belief systems from countless cultures. Indigenous American tribes spoke of subterranean peoples and worlds; Greek legends told of the Underworld; and Norse mythology mentioned Svartálfaheimr, a subterranean world inhabited by dwarves.

Their conceptualizations were models of the cosmos rather than scientific theories as we know them today. Yet, they remind us of humanity's enduring fascination with what might lie beneath the world we know.

9.2. Challenging the Paradigm: Edmund Halley's Hollow Earth

Long before the emergence of modern plate tectonics, the scientific community saw the Earth as a homogenous, solid entity. This paradigm took a turn with the arrival of Edmund Halley. Known for his prediction of Halley's Comet, he proposed an audacious theory in 1692 suggesting that the Earth was hollow, composed of multiple concentric shells separated by luminous atmospheres.

Halley's theory, though revolutionary, was built on shaky foundations, suggesting compass variations could be explained by the rotation of these inner concentric shells. He thought that the lights of the aurora borealis were a result of these inner atmospheres escaping through thin parts in the Earth's crust. Although largely inaccurate, his audacious hypothesis revealed science's growing readiness for unconventional ideas.

9.3. The Birth of Modern Geology: James Hutton and Charles Lyell

The field of study we now know as geology began its initial steps in the 18th and 19th centuries. During this time, James Hutton's revolutionary ideas made shockwaves across the scientific community. Known as the "Father of Modern Geology," he proposed deep time, implying the Earth was significantly older than previously thought. Human lifespan, he argued, was too short to witness Earth's vast geological changes, making it appear static.

With the passing baton to Charles Lyell in the 19th century, he refined Hutton's uniformitarianism principle, insisting that small, consistent processes like erosion or sediment deposition over a long period could cause substantial changes on Earth's surface. Lyell's work provided the foundation for Darwin's theory of evolution and painted a picture of an Earth shaped by its own internal and external processes over millions of years. But the question of what precisely drove these processes remained.

9.4. The Rise and Fall of the Expanding Earth Theory

Meanwhile, by the late 19th and early 20th century, some scientists proposed the Expanding Earth Theory. As the name suggests, adherents believed that the planet was slowly increasing in volume, explaining the shifting continental and oceanic features. The emergence of seafloor spreading and plate tectonics eventually led to this theory's decline. Though innovative at its time, it lacked a plausible mechanism for Earth's continuous expansion.

9.5. Birth of Plate Tectonics

The mid-20th century witnessed the rise of one of the most transformative geological theories: Plate Tectonics. Championed by Alfred Wegener in 1912, the theory of continental drift suggested that the continents ploughed through the oceans. The proposal was met with mockery and rebuttal due to its lack of a convincing motive mechanism. Yet, the discovery of seafloor spreading and paleomagnetic evidence in the 1960s transformed the ridiculed theory into the celebrated concept of Plate Tectonics.

This imaginative theory paints a portrait of our planet's lithosphere broken into several 'tectonic plates' that move relative to each other. These movements are responsible for earthquakes, volcanic activity, and the creation of geographic features such as mountains and oceanic trenches.

9.6. Just Scratching the Surface

After hundreds of years of scientific exploration, we have yet to penetrate more than a mere fraction of the Earth's crust. With the deepest borehole extending a little more than 12 kilometers, the rest of our knowledge about what lies deeper is based on our understanding of seismic waves. Though our journey has been fraught with missteps, each U-turn, from primordial myths and scientific theories to the prospects of the unknown, has brought us one step closer to understanding our home planet in its dynamic entirety.

In a nutshell, the tectonic plates on which we reside are akin to pieces on a cosmic chessboard, guided by the hidden hand of Earth's inner mechanisms. Despite our advances in technology and knowledge, the enigma of our planet's interior continues to challenge scientists, igniting exploratory zeal as hot as the mantle itself. The deeper we probe into the Earth, the more we discover about our own existence and the evolutionary saga of the planet we call home.

Chapter 10. Let there be Light: The Phenomenon of Central Sun

Guiding our journey to the core of Earth, it is perhaps fitting to begin with a strange, yet widely reported phenomenon – the concept of a Central Sun. Often associated with pseudoscience or the realm of myths, this notion has piqued the curiosity of thinkers from all walks of life. But, to fathom this bright enigma, we must delve into its many origins and dimensions: the snippets of stories, tales, theories, and chronicles associated with it.

10.1. Inside Illumination

Despite its fantastical impression, the idea of 'internal illumination' has been prevalent in various forms across civilizations. The aboriginal cave paintings of Australia hint at 'bright beings' dwelling in Earth's womb. Similarly, both Greek and Roman lore casually speak of the Underworld illuminated by a mysterious light source.

Intriguingly, some Inuit cultures in the Arctic Circle, have oral traditions speaking of a warm land within Earth where the Sun never sets. They claim their ancestors had descended from this illuminated sanctuary. While these stories may easily be dismissed as folktales, their consistency cannot be entirely neglected.

This unlikely consistency peaked in the 19th-century Hollow Earth Theory. Pioneered by Captain John Cleves Symmes Jr., the theory posited that planet Earth was not a solid ball but consisted of several concentric shells with an accessible interior void. Symmes went on to proclaim this internal realm harbored its light source – an Inner Sun.

10.2. The Hollow Earth Theory: Light from Within

Symmes, a war veteran, spent considerable efforts promoting his model of the Hollow Earth. He drafted numerous diagrams explaining the configuration, which he claimed were based on scientific principles of the day. The Inner Sun was postulated as being suspended in the center, supplying the inner earth with both light and warmth.

Symmes believed the inner earth was inhabited, potentially by beings far advanced than those on the surface. He proposed that this central luminary was responsible for the northern and southern lights – what we know now as the Aurora Borealis and Aurora Australis. He suggested these phenomena were a result of the Inner Sun's light leaking from pole openings leading to the Earth's interior.

10.3. Between Myth and Science: The Scientific Positings

Despite ridicule from the scientific community, the Hollow Earth Theory spurred a wave of literary and exploratory excitement. Jules Verne's "Journey to the Center of the Earth" and Edgar Allan Poe's "MS. Found in a Bottle" are noteworthy examples. However, Symmes' models are significant, despite their eventual debunking, as they spurred discussions on earth's geology and led to the development of more rigorous analysis techniques.

The Inner Sun notion has persisted, fueled further by the alleged secret diary of Admiral Richard Byrd. Byrd, a polar explorer, purportedly wrote of flying into the Earth's interior where he encountered advanced civilizations and lush vegetation – all under the glow of an Inner Sun.

Though unfounded and widely regarded as a hoax, Byrd's tales bring us to a critical juncture – the blurred zone between myth and science. Science should not blindly follow or outrightly dismiss such ideas. Instead, underlying principles should be extracted, analyzed, and validated.

10.4. The Hard Evidence: Case of Geothermal Energy

For instance, let's consider the mechanism proposed for the Inner Sun. Symmes theorized it operated similar to our known Sun, through nuclear fusion. While this aspect is suspect, it indirectly touches upon the proven principle of geothermal energy – the Earth does emit heat from its core. Herein, we find a compelling correlation and a learning opportunity.

The Earth's core is extremely hot, reaching temperatures similar to the surface of the Sun. This heat is produced by radioactive decay in the Earth's mantle. While not producing light, this is a form of energy transmission. Earth's inner heat drives tectonic plate movement, volcanic activity, and is the basis for geothermal energy systems. In this way, there is a 'sun' within our Earth, not of light but of heat.

10.5. The Phenomena of Bioluminescence: Life in the Deep Dark

Parallel to this idea is the remarkable adaptation by certain deep-sea creatures. Some species living in the dark abyss of the oceans have developed bioluminescence – the ability to produce and emit light. This natural 'living light' brightens up the ocean depths under miles of dark waters, symbolizing life's dexterity to create its lighting systems where the sun's rays can't reach.

Could similar adaptations have evolved within Earth's unknown depths? As we continue our exciting exploration, the chapters ahead will further test the boundaries of this scientific possibility.

While science has not yet affirmed a radiant central sun within the Earth, an in-depth examination reveals aspects that stimulate intellectual curiosity. From the myths peeping through the annals of civilizations, tales of explorers, to the realities of geothermal heat and bioluminescence, the concept of an Inner Sun permeates various dimensions, fueling our fascination of the world beneath us. By reflecting on these insights, we come to understand that the 'Inner Sun', in the lyrical or literal sense, might be more of a testament to the enduring spirit of inquiry that lights the way towards expanding our understanding of our home planet.

Chapter 11. Into the Future: Ongoing Exploration and Speculative Concepts

The promise of the future carries the essence of exploring the unknown within it. For millennia, humans have looked toward the stars for this sense of exploration, yet so much remains undiscovered beneath our feet. As we journey inwards, speculating about concepts beyond our current reach, we can only imagine the wonders and mysteries which might be unveiled in the unfolding eras of our civilization.

11.1. Journey to the Core: Quantum Mechanics and Earth's Heart

To understand the inscrutabilities of the Earth's interior, we must turn to quantum physics. Quantum mechanics, a pillar of modern physics, infers that reality on subatomic levels behaves wildly different from what our intuition deems possible. The future may see its principles applied in groundbreaking ways to dredge up the secrets encapsulated in the Earth's core.

Think of the Earth's core as a chest of mysteries, locked by extreme pressures and temperatures, with the key being this unique field of study. Quantum tunneling, a phenomenon wherein particles 'jump' through physical barriers, might eventually be harnessed as a tool for reaching our planet's elusive heart. Scientists of tomorrow may not require physically piercing into the mantle and the core, but instead could 'tunnel' their ways, gathering data about the very material the Earth's heart is made of, using meticulously developed quantum technologies.

The development of such technology, however speculative it may seem, promises revolutionary insights. Are there compounds under such extreme conditions that could lend themselves to unprecedented technological advancements, just awaiting discovery? Or perhaps, an energy source unbeknownst to our current understanding of physics? These questions are part and parcel of what drives the next generation of explorers forward.

11.2. Seismic Waves: Unveiling the Layered World

Seismology, the study of earthquakes and the waves they produce, has allowed us to form the current scientific understanding of the Earth's interior. The analysis of seismic waves provides us with an effective, albeit indirect, method of peering beneath our footsteps. Future advancements in this field could significantly improve our interpretation of how seismic waves interface with various layers.

Imagine seismic waves as echoes used by bats for navigation. As the wave radiates through different materials, their velocities change, and some are reflected back. Increased precision in recording and analyzing seismic wave propagation could generate exceptional 3D models of Earth's subsurface, including the intricate labyrinth of tectonic plate boundaries that exists more than a hundred kilometers below the surface.

11.3. Hollow Earth Theory: Science or Pseudoscience

The so-called 'Hollow Earth' theory, originally the imagination's child playing with scientific ideas, has been both denied and vouched for, making it the subject of much debate over centuries. The idea postulates a hollow Earth filled with life, conjecturing an interior sun that lights up a utopian civilization at the heart of our planet. Traversing from myth to pseudoscience, this topic has been a recurring trendy speculation. Nonetheless, serious scientific exploration of these conjectures is sparse, largely owing to seismic wave data that indicate a solid Earth.

However, reflecting on its past may illuminate paths into the future. While the traditional Hollow Earth theory is regarded as primordial pseudoscience, it may inspire more pragmatic research questions pertaining to subsurface cavities—vast, hitherto undiscovered. There already are documented caves extending thousands of meters below ground. Future research might discover exceedingly colossal cavities, potentially having unique ecosystems, sheltering exotic life, and harboring untapped resources.

11.4. The Speculative Frontier: Towards the Future

Perhaps the future will see us mapping the labyrinths of magma reservoirs, or complex networks of gigantic underground aquifers, or even unveiling mysterious bio-complexes beneath our feet, resembling science fiction ecosystems. The possibilities are endless—such is the beauty of speculative future concepts.

From the quantum mechanics' 'tunneling' to the Earth's heart, to advanced seismic research letting us 'see' beneath the crust, and challenging pseudoscientific ideas driving us towards further exploration—the future appears overwhelmingly exciting. Not only are we becoming adept at understanding our planet but also developing a profound respect for the beauty it holds within.

We find ourselves at the threshold of unimaginable discoveries. The planet Earth, in its majestic scale and complexity, remains an unsolved puzzle despite our ceaseless explorations. But with each forward step in science and technology, the mysteries of the inner

Earth become less formidable, promising a future of awe-inspiring revelations.

We stand upon the cusp of a new age—an age of humankind, embarking on an unprecedented journey towards the center of our home, unravelling truth piece by piece, layer by layer. The mysteries of the Earth are waiting for us, and it is the relentless pursuit of knowledge that shall illuminate our way. The smoky clouds of uncertainty that hide the Earth's true nature are dissipating as we advance, and all we have to do is look forward—with an unquenched curiosity—to what lies ahead.

For it is often in the darkest skies that we see the brightest stars. And under the heaviest rocks might just lie the most priceless gems. Such is the journey into the Future: Ongoing Exploration and Speculative Concepts—a journey into the uncertain, a journey towards enlightenment. The future is, indeed, a fascinating place to venture into.

www.ingramcontent.com/pod-product-compliance
Lightning Source LLC
LaVergne TN
LVHW051634050326
832903LV00033B/4753